SINGING OVER HAVERING

Bob and Mary Bain

OPEN WELLS PUBLISHING

Copyright 2017 by Bob and Mary Bain

All rights reserved

This book or any portion thereof may not be reproduced or used in any manner whatsoever without the express written permission of the publisher except for the use of brief quotations in a book review or scholarly journal.

ISBN 978-1-326-96370-5

London, United Kingdom

Bob and Mary Bain

e-mail:bobbain@hotmail.co.uk

CONTENTS

PART ONE SINGING OVER HAVERING - THE VISION

1 Joining in with Creation's Song……………...………9
2 Opening the Door for God's Presence…………………13
3 One Day, Eighty Worshippers, Eight Locations……….15
4 My Song Matters……………………………………….19
5 Making a Way for Worship……………………………23

PART TWO LOOKING AT THE EIGHT LOCATIONS

1 Havering-Atte-Bower - God's Royal Place…………….27
2 Romford – God's Spacious Place………………………..35
3 The Two Harolds - God's Honoured Place…..………….39
4 Hornchurch - God's Place of Power……..…………….45
5 Upminster - God's Holy Place………………………….51
6 Elm Park - God's Place of Hope………………………...53
7 Rainham – God's Remembering Place………………….57
8 The Eighth Place, Collier Row - God's Hidden Place…..61

PART THREE GRASSROOTS AND OPEN WELLS

Grassroots and Open Wells…………………………………….73

Some References………………………………………………77

INTRODUCTION

'You shall go out with joy and be led forth with peace and the mountains and the hills shall break forth into song before you' (Isaiah 55:12)

This book is for all those who are interested in how God is doing things in the London Borough of Havering. We felt compelled to chronicle something. We wanted to write down on tablets what we have been seeing so that others can run with it (Hab. 2:2). In particular this book is a written encouragement for you to sing out songs from the Lord over the land in which you live.

Front Cover Photograph: Bluebells
We have been made Heavenly bells to ring out and sing out God's song of liberty over Havering.

PART ONE

SINGING OVER HAVERING

The Vision

CHAPTER ONE
JOINING IN WITH CREATION'S SONG

Wherever you are living, you have a unique song to sing there from the Lord. At the start of creation Job records that, as the Lord sunk the bases and laid the cornerstone, the morning stars sang together and the sons of God shouted for joy (Job 38:7). The stars sang together and from that beginning the whole of creation continues to resonate. The Lord's creative energy still continues to vibrate in its every atom and molecule, showing His glory. An amazing creation song is going up all the time and we have the privilege of consciously joining in with the choir. As one great worshipper, Godfrey Birtill says, when people come to hear him, 'Don't go criticising the band – we're all the band!' In Romans chapter eight, Paul tells us that the whole of creation groans, waiting for the appearance of the sons of God. No wonder then that in the words of Isaiah, the mountains and the hills break forth into song before us, even when we are out and about doing the most ordinary things.

Looking into London

The land where Mary and I have been living over the last eight years is the London Borough of Havering. It lies on the East side of London and is one of thirty-two city boroughs which, along with the City of London itself, govern the capital. Havering is at the very edge of London. Five minutes drive up the road going out, and you are in open countryside and rural Essex farms. Going into the city centre, you can drive through a continuous urban environment for seventeen miles. From the high points in Havering you can see all the way in to London. There is Canary Wharf, there is the Shard and there is even a glimpse of the London Eye. At night it is a spectacular view. On Bonfire Night and New Year's Eve it is an even more amazing sight as fireworks shoot off into the night sky. During the 2012 Olympics which were centred in London's east end, the military took over the top of Highfield Towers, a solitary block of flats on top of one of the highest points in Havering. It acted as an observation post against terror attacks. Militarily speaking, Havering is London's Eastgate, guarding its eastern approaches.

An invitation from God

There are about two hundred and fifty thousand people in Havering, and in the adjoining Boroughs there are similar numbers – millions of people within a few miles of each other.
God wants to bring His salvation to the whole area. He loves each one of Havering's two hundred and fifty thousand, and cries out for each of us to be reconciled to Him. The death of Jesus on the cross has made this possible and He is no longer counting our sins against us (2 Cor.5:19). He invites us to repent, to change our minds and cross from death to life. He invites us to pick up His songbook and sing a new song from the Lord to the whole of creation.

It's time to sing out

This is what we felt God was telling us to do in Havering. Firstly we were to map the place from God's perspective and pick out the highest points in the Borough. Then we were to go to them and sing, even if it was just the two of us, Mary and I. The words of the old hymn came to mind – 'Softly and tenderly Jesus is calling... Come home'. There was a sense that we were to call out to every soul in Havering, 'Return to the Lord, Come Home to Him.' We felt God saying, 'This is the time'.

The Vision

We were to take worship teams plus a mix of other people from local churches to different spots and 'flash mob' sing at them on the same day, all at the same time. We were to gather others we already knew to help who had caught the same kind of vision for Havering. Two of these helpers were Sean Gooch and Sam Hayley. Sean Gooch has been faithfully gathering worshippers together over the last few years, for a monthly BURN. The vision of BURN across the world is of worshippers spending an evening, or a whole night, in worship, burning with the love of God in their local areas. Sam Hayley, along with others has been regularly hosting an open praise evening on one Sunday each month, open to everyone across the borough.

Proclaiming freedom

We felt that God was saying 'sing from the mountaintop' in a prophetic releasing way, proclaiming God's Kingdom has come, and we would be given the anointing to do this task. Jesus was inviting us to join in the declaring out of His commission, and this would be our commission too. In the words of Luke chapter four, 'The Spirit of the Lord is upon me because He has anointed me, to preach the gospel to the poor. He has sent me to heal the broken-hearted, to proclaim liberty to the captives and recovery of sight to the blind, to set at liberty those who are oppressed, to proclaim the acceptable year of the Lord'.

Taking the High Places

We were being called to take the 'high places', the places in opposition to God. The old chorus expresses it well, 'With the high praises of God in our mouth and a two-edged sword in our hands, we'll march right on to the Victory side, right into Canaan's land'.

CHAPTER TWO
OPENING THE DOOR FOR GOD'S PRESENCE

An open door has always spoken to me [Mary] about welcome, about being included and invited in. When I became a Christian it was in part through reading a leaflet that included the scripture 'Behold I stand at the door and knock. If anyone hears my voice and opens the door, I will come in and eat with him and he with me.' (Rev.3:20). In the context of this passage God declares that He is standing knocking at the door of the church in Laodicea, and giving them the opportunity to open the door and welcome Him in. This passage isn't just a message for the church in Laodicea, but a message to the church in whichever area you live. For the church in Havering, God is standing knocking at the door and waiting for us to invite His presence in. This is a personal invitation, but it is also one given to the whole church.

What a crazy thought that we might actually ever consider getting on with things and not including Him. This would be major insanity. How we would miss out if we were crazy enough to leave Him at the door. As we sit down, and have fellowship with Him, an intimacy grows, and our thoughts and desires unite with His. We start to think like Jesus thinks, and then, when we go out and do things, we are truly being His hands and feet on the earth. He never intended it to be otherwise.

A place of revival
We can declare today that Havering is a place of revival, because we have opened the door to God's presence, and He has come in. The change that has begun in our innermost parts

– the intimacy of our relationship with Him, is spreading out and touching the whole body of Christ in this area. It is affecting our families, our streets, the Borough and the capital, even the whole nation.

My home town, Hull has just been declared the UK City of Culture 2017. [Bob] Growing up there and knowing the place as a child, my first thought on hearing the news was 'Who would have thought it!' Even now, I'm thinking that this declaration may be more aspirational and a work in progress rather than an accomplished reality. Who am I to say? However the representatives of Hull must have got together and filled in the application forms, and the City of Culture officials must have responded to the application, visited the city and decided it could be declared this year's UK City of Culture. Well, in the same way, here is the church in Havering, and you can be sure that God has heard those in His church who have prayed, 'Your Kingdom come, Your will be done on Earth, in Havering as it is in Heaven'. He is a generous God and has taken us at our word. We have filled in our 'application form' for God's will to be done in Havering as it is in Heaven, and He has generously responded to our request.

God has declared Havering a place where His will is done. In the same way that Hull is being called the UK city of culture and I can hardly believe it, some may consider God's declaration over Havering to be rather more aspirational and a work in progress than an accomplished reality. But who are we to argue with God? Isn't this what faith is, and what God is good at doing? He calls those things that are not as though they are, and amazingly in doing so they become so! With confidence then we can declare Havering to be a place of revival.

CHAPTER THREE
ONE DAY, EIGHTY WORSHIPPERS, EIGHT LOCATIONS

In the late afternoon of Sunday 7th June 2015, seventy to eighty representative worshippers, pray<u>ers</u> and prophets sang at eight different locations around the London Borough of Havering. My wife, Mary and I were two of them. Our vision to sing over Havering had become a reality! The pace of the Holy Spirit is such that a date, only a short while back, can seem like pre-history, but God holds all our tears in a bottle and numbers the days and the years, and we believe that this date goes down as a significant one.

We chose certain places from which the groups would sing, declare and pray. This doesn't mean that there aren't other significant places in the Borough, but just that these were the 'high places' which God highlighted for us on this particular occasion.

Physical maps and Spiritual landscapes
The Ordnance Survey originally mapped the British countryside for military purposes using trig points. These were carefully chosen points in the landscape which, when measured in relation to one another, provided the framework for the bigger picture. Their work had to start with getting the positions for the Trig points accurately located. Eventually, a whole map was built up which now serves many other purposes beyond its original military intentions. Just as the OS originally mapped Havering using prominent trig points so we can also look for spiritual markers, to help us understand the spiritual landscape.

Looking into the spiritual landscape
What does this landscape look like? We need to pray a prayer like Elisha's for his young servant in 2 Kings 6:17. He prayed, 'Lord, open his eyes that he may see'. The Lord heard the prayer, and 'behold the mountain was full of horses and chariots of fire round about Elisha'. Suddenly the young man was in a very different landscape.

Havering is no different. There is a lot more going on than what an OS map can show. With spiritually open eyes, the geography of Havering is a very different landscape. This landscape is full of people, and full of people's prayers. It is wrapped around with His decrees and commandments, and vibrates with worship. There are memorial stones telling stories of what has gone before, and crossroads where decisions have been made. Angels are stationed in various places, others are on the move. There are baptisms, and there is bread and wine. This landscape contains the fullness of everything, and is the one we are all journeying through.

Walking through the landscape
As we look around there are people walking in the light and walking by faith; walking with wisdom and walking in love. It is a mobile, fluid landscape. Changes are going on all the time as we walk through the places in which we live. People's lives are changing, even as a result of our being there. Out of the dark places, lives are being touched by God's presence and lined up with His will, and salvation is coming to the people of Havering.

Singing out God's heart
The Holy Spirit is blowing all over the place. The church in Havering is there with Him, moving around in the geography. Everything is quite wild and yet very orderly, all at the same

time. We keep being positioned, and re-positioned by God, potted, and then re-potted, to make a difference and to bring His blessing to the whole community. He is sharing with us His heart for the area and we are singing this out, in songs, declarations and prayers, and the landscape and the people are changing, as God's will is sung out.

God on the move

In this moving landscape there may be some steady markers but mostly things are on the move. Recently, we were involved in making a film about what God has been doing in the Havering area. There were so many things happening over a single year, that the film could only provide an encouraging snapshot. 'God on the move' was an apt title for the film. During the year, people were coming and going, some things stopped and new things were bubbling up. There was nothing static about this spiritual landscape - it had a time dimension to it.

Moving in the Spirit in Havering

CHAPTER FOUR
MY SONG MATTERS

Everyone of us carries a different song but everyone's song matters! It might not be considered important by others, but in the bigger picture it's all important to God. My personality creates a sound. The word, Person, by which we describe ourselves, even has its roots in sound. It is a Latin compound word coming from, 'per' meaning through, and 'sonic' meaning sound. We are beings through which sound comes. Every new-born baby is a witness to this truth!

David's intimate song

Psalm 119 is a wonderful psalm of celebration by David. It uses the twenty-two letters of the Hebrew alphabet in sequence to make twenty-two sections, each starting with a new letter. Section by section, David describes his own journey through the spiritual landscape set before him. This is his own intimate song through the alphabet of his life. His responses are sung out, as he ponders on the wonders of God's word and lives out God's declared decrees, engraved into his life. There are some moments when he cried out in particular situations, and stepped out in God's commanded direction. Others where he gave deep thanks for God's precepts (that help which God had already put within him, and which had followed him all the days of his life). He remembers and praises God's testimonies, the stories of God's goodness that each step of his life was creating. Through the whole psalm, he sings out of his experience of being wrapped around, and governed by the flow of God's law.

Songs that still resonate today

David's song to the Lord, and the songs that other people were singing out in later generations still resonate today! They are bringing layers of beauty and loveliness into what is unfolding now, alongside our own songs too. Together we create a Song of Songs, brilliantly orchestrated by God for His glory. Zephaniah 3:17 reads, The Lord your God is with you, He is mighty to save. He will take great delight in you, He will quiet you with His love, He will rejoice over you with singing'. Through the generations God has been singing over us, and through us.

Coming together in harmony

Our songs matter. Every part in the choir is needed. In 1 Corinthians chapter twelve Paul strongly warns us that in the body of Jesus Christ we are all necessary. No-one is to be considered redundant.

'Spem in aliem' is a motet composed by Thomas Tallis, around 1570, for eight choirs of five voices each – that's forty parts in all, making up the most amazing sound from an awful lot of voices. The theme of the motet translates from the Latin as 'I have never put my hope in any other but in You, O God of Israel'. Our sentiment exactly. It is God in whom we hope. He is the great composer who beats Thomas Tallis in making a good song out of the lot of us.

The people who sang out on that special Sunday in June 2015 were drawn from worship teams who had previously met up with each other. Earlier that year, in April, we had organised a gathering of Havering worship teams, not to practice for an event, but just to get to know one another. At the start of the day, we played 'Spem in aliem' to make the point that the Lord was bringing us together in a wonderful relational harmony. Many parts were being brought together, to express His glory across the whole Borough. A word given to the worship team from the Church of the Good Shepherd, by a Singaporean brother, when visiting their church, is a word for us all. He prayed over them, and said that they were 'bringing in the colours and sounds of Heaven'.

My Song Matters

My song matters
I have a song and I need to sing it.
My song makes a difference in the world
To those around me.
You are making me, and shaping me, and forming me -
So I can sing the song of Mary; (insert your own name!)
The song of my life with You.

Telling all that You have done
And all that You are doing-
A beautiful melody
With some painful notes
But many sweet moments...
A song of victory over sin,
Overcoming evil,
And pushing through in joy!
A triumph,
Unglimpsed by many,
But totally appreciated by You
And a few...
Who know me better!

Help me to sing the song,
Expressing all the joy
You have put in me.
All the investment
Is appreciated...
I know that I am loved by You

(from 'My Song Matters – A book of Poems' by Mary Bain)

CHAPTER FIVE
MAKING A WAY FOR WORSHIP

Opening the doors and repairing them
How is revival being nurtured in Havering? There is Biblical precedence that it starts with the worshippers and the prophets. We see in 1 Chronicles chapter 29 for example, under their new king Hezekiah, the start of something of a revival for the nation of Israel. It begins with him opening the doors of the disused Temple and repairing them. His father, king Ahaz had locked the doors during his reign and had angered the Lord by worshipping idols instead (2 Chron. 28:22-25). Now Hezekiah, by opening the doors of the Temple, was making a way for the people to come back to worship the Lord. Once more the singers and the musicians could be stationed in the way commanded by the Lord, and everything re-established, according to the words given through the prophets.

Prophetic worship begins
Not only was everything done according to the words of the prophets, David's instructions, in 1 Chronicles chapter 25 also describe the singers themselves as having 'the ministry of prophesying accompanied by harps, lyres and cymbals'. Elsewhere they are described as ministering before the ark, making petition, giving thanks and praising the Lord. (1 Chron 16:4) This is a wide brief indeed. When all was completed, Hezekiah made the appeal for the people to return to the Lord, and celebrate the great feast of the Passover (2 Chron. 29:25-28). The Passover appeal went out, 'Come and celebrate the Lord who delivered you from your enemy and brought you into a new life!' The people came, and the whole land woke up to revival. Nurturing revival, in a place of revival, starts with opening the doors of the temple for prophetic worship to begin.

Willing hearts open to change
But when the doors were opened what did Hezekiah see? All the rubbish and the mess that had been left inside! So the king called together a group of leaders, those with willing hearts, to do the work of clearing out the temple. But first a personal cleansing was needed. Isn't it interesting that God always begins with our hearts? Just as opening the doors of the temple revealed the rubbish inside, so when we open our hearts to God, things change in His presence. The prayer rises up within us, in the words of Psalm 51:7-11 'Create in me a clean heart, O God, and renew a right spirit within me'. We hear the knock on the door, we invite Jesus in, and as we sit down and eat with Him, and are open and transparent with Him, a wonderful cleansing goes on.

Intimacy changes us
We are being changed by this journey of intimacy and when it's all over, we are not the same people. Two of our sons, not that long ago, completed the Pennine Way, a long distance trail that they walked over sixteen or so days. There is a pub in the village, at the end of the walk on the Scottish border, which offers every walker completing the walk a free half-pint of beer. 'How do you know we've done the walk?' was the question they asked the man behind the bar. His response was, 'We take one look at you, and we know you've done it!' In the same way, the journey of intimacy causes us to change and become more like the One we love. People will notice that we are different. Revival in Havering is being nurtured through our intimacy with Jesus.

PART TWO

LOOKING AT THE EIGHT LOCATIONS

PART TWO

LOOKING AFTER SIGHT LOCATIONS

PLACE ONE

HAVERING-ATTE-BOWER - GOD'S ROYAL PLACE

At the highest point in the Borough, at 105m above sea level, is the village of Havering-atte-Bower This is where the royal palace of the last Saxon king, Harold, was sited, and earlier where another king, Edward the Confessor also lived. From the village green, you can see why this spot was chosen for the royal palace. There are tremendous views down the eight miles or so to the River Thames southwards, and also westwards, all the way into the middle of London. The high vantage point also gives it a strong military position, from which the whole Borough of Havering can be viewed.

God's overview and battle plans

On Sunday 7th June 2015, the Green at Havering-atte-Bower was one of the places from which we chose to sing. It is a significant location because it reminds us that the Lord has His own strategies and battle plans for our area. The earthly royal palace has been and gone, and the battle plans of earthly kings with it, but of course God's plans continue. Peter tells us, in 2 Peter chapter two, that we are a chosen people, a royal priesthood, a holy nation, a people belonging to God that we might declare the praises of Him who called us out of darkness, into His wonderful light. We see ourselves as royalty, like King Harold and King Edward, declaring God's praises, together with the King of Kings, over our borough of Havering.

Speaking out blessing

In Jeremiah 29:11, promises are spoken out to the people of Israel. These are plans to bless, and not to harm, plans to bring peace and give a good future. We can speak these promises out for our community. As we, the people of God who live in Havering, seek its prosperity, we are being the good salt and light that Jesus called us to be. In this place, we can also speak out Jesus' words of blessing, describing His (and our) mission. 'The Spirit of the Lord is upon me because He has anointed me to preach the gospel to the poor. He has sent me to heal the broken-hearted, to proclaim liberty to the captives and recovery of sight to the blind, to set at liberty those who are oppressed, to proclaim the acceptable year of the Lord' (Luke 4:18-19).

Our royal position of authority
From God's heavenly throne room and vantage point, just like from the royal palace at Havering-atte-Bower, the detailed plans and assignments for our area are being ordered. As members of His royal family, we are there with Him in the throne room, to hear and to do our part. He is King over the battle – He sees, declares and determines the outcome of the war. He wants us to be with Him in the Throne room, and to understand His strategy. This is the place where wars are won. In Ephesians chapter two, Paul tells us that God has raised us up with Christ and seated us with Him, in the heavenly realms, in Christ Jesus. In chapter one, we are told that this is a place of authority 'far above all rule and authority, power and dominion and every title that can be given, not only in the present age but in the one to come'.

Standing and waiting in prayer
On one occasion in Israel's history, faced with an attack on the nation which was overwhelming, the king, Jehoshaphat, gathered the people in prayer. His prayer establishes who God is. In 2 Chron. 20 we read, 'O Lord, God of our fathers, are you not the God who is in Heaven? You rule over all the

kingdoms of the nations. Power and might are in your hand and no-one can withstand you.' He ended his prayer with the words, 'We do not know what to do but <u>our eyes are upon you.</u>' After he had prayed, the prophetic word of reassurance and direction came as the people stood there, waiting before the Lord. God told them that they would not have to fight this battle but they were to march down against the enemy and see the deliverance that the Lord would give them.

The worshippers go in front

The next morning, the king appointed men to sing to the Lord, as they went out, at the head of the army. As they began to sing praises to God, the Lord went up ahead of them all and saw to it that the vast army of the enemy was destroyed. When the worshippers finally got to the spot where they could look down over the enemy, there was no enemy left to fight!

A royal bride as well as a royal priesthood

Just slightly down the hill from the village of Havering-atte-Bower sits Bower House. This is positioned on the historic site of the Saxon queen's quarters, and is now a Christian training centre. The name, Bower may refer to the Saxon bride's bedchamber. It is a good reminder that the Church is not only a royal priesthood but also a royal bride, called to dwell close to her king. This may be something for the students at Bower House to consider while they are about their studies! We are the Lord's royal bride, and He loves to respond to the voice of His beloved as we call out to Him.

God is watching over His word

God's words are spoken out like seed, bearing fruit in our lives. Not one word returns void to the throne room of God. Every word accomplishes what was intended (Isa. 55:11) He is calling us into fruitfulness, through His word inside us. This was God's reassurance to the young prophet, Jeremiah, that He would watch over His word to fulfil it. (Jer.1:12). There is a play on words in the passage – God presents a vision of an almond branch to Jeremiah, to drive the point home that He will fulfil His words, because the word for almond in Hebrew sounds like the word for watching.

Inspired by this story of God calling Jeremiah to begin to prophesy, there is a whole genre of art called <u>mandorlas</u> (which is the Latin word for almond). These paintings are always shaped like an almond. They revisit that Jeremiah moment, and seek to reassure us that the Lord still continues to fulfil the words He has spoken. Chelmsford Cathedral, in our local Anglican diocese, has an example. On the wall is a large almond-shaped painting of God sitting enthroned, watching over His word. Mandorlas, elsewhere, sometimes have a symbolic depiction of the four gospels, the ox, the man, the lion and the eagle, around God's throne. This also reminds us of Ezekiel's description of God's glory, in Ezekiel chapter one, when he sees the four living creatures around the throne of God, each bearing the faces of an ox, a man, a lion and an eagle. The mandorla in Chelmsford really emphasizes the point that, even in our local area, God is indeed on His throne, presiding over His plans and purposes, and watching over His words to fulfil them.

God's question for Havering

The question, Jeremiah was invited to answer was, <u>What do you see?</u> This is also God's question to us for Havering, What do we see? What do we see regarding Havering? We can only successfully answer this question by seeing through the eyes of the Spirit, and then declaring out what we see, trusting that we are part of the process through which God will fulfil His words. We can declare 'Tomorrow can be different', to borrow a motto from one of our local churches - the Church of the Good Shepherd, because God has declared it so.

Seeing and declaring in the Spirit

When we start to answer questions like, What do you see?, we can get some surprises! Prophetic statements can be very subjective. Words, visions, dreams and pictures are seen and heard, and then interpreted and delivered through the human agency. This gives wide scope for variation, even if we set aside outright errors and inaccuracies. In one sense, we can choose what we see, or at least how we see it. It's possible to walk distracted and blinkered through the landscape, and not really take in what we are seeing. Just like when you are driving on a motorway in automatic, and listening to the radio. The content of the radio is what you're taking in, not the scenery. In another sense, our capacity to understand what we see, and our breadth of vocabulary will shape our ability to describe. However, we are seeing <u>something</u>; we are hearing <u>something</u>. God isn't a minimalist and gives us plenty to see and hear. Why not? Our Heavenly Father delights to communicate with His children and you can be sure He has things to say to us on a daily basis, even if it is just to say, I love you.

Humbly trust in God's leading

For those hearing and receiving words from others, no absolute proof of their truth is possible, or the breadth of their applicability. This might seem a little frustrating for those who like everything to be very clear and very absolute. We are left only with indicators as to how true they are. We may have gut feelings as to whether words given to an individual have a wider relevance, but this is hardly proof. By indicators, I mean this kind of thing. You might have personally got a word yourself that day along similar lines, and then later on picked up on the theme, in a general conversation with someone at a shop. Maybe God is bringing something to your attention. The co-incidences pile up, and you recognise something is going on. What can be done to give you a sense of certainty? Externally, not a lot. There is only one real safeguard, and that is a humble reliance on God, a trust that He has the ability to lead you by His Spirit.

Isaiah 57:19 tells us that God lives 'in a high and holy place but also with the one who is contrite and lowly in spirit'. We trust that you will let the Holy Spirit in you help you to weigh up the different words of this book, and their significance, as presented here.

A stronger liberty

Havering was declared a royal liberty in 1465 by Edward IV who was king at the time, confirming the privileges that had already grown up around the royal palace. For Havering, this secured the area as a tax haven, and for many centuries it remained independent of the control of Essex or London.

Havering's coat of arms

No taxes had to be paid at all. It had its own commercial market and local justice system. The coat of arms for the London Borough of Havering still declares out the word, 'Liberty' to commemorate this period.

Jesus has declared a stronger Liberty across Havering. This is a freedom for the oppressed, that goes far beyond liberty from the taxman, and a few marketplace privileges. Fundamentally, Jesus has cut through the shroud of death caused by our sin, and released us into His new life. Those who hear His words of liberty, and receive them, are forever free, royal children who sing out the words, 'Abba Father'.

PLACE TWO
ROMFORD - GOD'S SPACIOUS PLACE

The name Romford is derived, according to most authorities, from the Old English and means 'spacious or roomy ford'. I love the meaning of the name and it reminds me that God invites us into a new place with Him, that is truly a spacious place. Psalm 18 tells us, 'He brought me out into a spacious place; He rescued me because He delighted in me'. We read in Genesis twenty-six of Isaac's troubles with the Philistines. He re-opens old wells and digs new ones, but at each one he finds himself in quarrels and disputes with the Philistines. Finally a new well is dug, and no-one quarrels over it. He names it Rehoboth which means spaciousness, saying, 'Now the Lord has given us room and we will flourish in the land'. Romford expresses God's expansiveness. He wants us to know that His is a spacious place, in which there is plenty of room for everyone to move around.

The centre shifted
Romford lies on the main communication route between Colchester and London, and has been a through route for commerce into the capital since Roman times. However Romford hasn't always been in the same spot! What was the centre of Romford shifted by 1410, from an area south of the present railway station, now known as Oldchurch, because of flooding. The new church of St Edward the Confessor was built at this time, and the old St Andrew's chapel in Oldchurch abandoned. The new centre became the market place on the London to Colchester road and the present High Street. When the railway line came through, a station was opened in 1839, further down South Street, back towards the site of the old

centre. This shifted the commercial centre again, this time towards the station, so that the main shopping street ended up stretching all along South Street, between the two important East-West routes into London - the road and the railway station. A lot of shifting has gone on!

Spiritual shifts in what God is doing

We chose South Street as a significant place to sing because it was a place that had seen a lot of shifting over the years. God does different things at different seasons, now, and through the generations. Just as the commercial centre of Romford has shifted several times at different points in history, it shouldn't surprise us when things shift in the Spirit. Romford hasn't stayed the same physically, and neither should we expect it to stay the same spiritually. South Street, as the present commercial centre of the town, has come about as a result of a number of historic developments. God is likewise ordering the developments that go on, in the spiritual geography of Havering. We need to understand the times and seasons and move accordingly, as the Spirit of God directs us. We want to be ready and expectant for changes, in the things that God is doing in Havering.

Spiritual provision

We also chose to sing from the middle of Romford, outside Marks and Spencers, to express something about commerce. Romford has been throughout its history a <u>gateway place of provision</u> for the city. Commerce has flowed through here. Cattle have been corralled in its marketplace, on their way to feeding the population of the capital. We are praying that this flow of commerce will be a godly flow. The enemy wants a different kind of Romford that trades destructively, in a pleasure-seeking lifestyle of drugs and drink. This is a deadening flow that has led to despair and suicide. God's provision brings life in abundance.

God is doing a good thing

Here are the words of Matt Carter, as he recalls growing up in Romford not that long ago.

'So with Havering, I'm reminded of in the Bible where it says, No good thing can come out of Nazareth! And when you know Romford, I remember when I was younger, when I was in my teens and I used to read magazines [and one magazine] had a picture of the Hulk, and it was the Hulk being really angry, and it said, 'A regular night out in Romford'. Now this is a magazine that is published all around the UK. But people knew Romford to be a place which was rough. I worked in London, and I had people from West London coming to Romford for a crazy night! So ... What good thing can come from Romford? What good thing can come from Havering? But you know what, God is doing a good thing in Havering. It is not just happening elsewhere, or outside, it is happening right here, and that's to God's glory because it's got to be God... and I love that! So in the darkness, the light shines brighter'.

Guarding the gateway

Marks and Spencers trades under the brand, St Michael's. We felt this was an appropriate shop from which to sing, because St.Michael traditionally is seen as the angel who guards what God is doing through His people! God has stationed His angels across the commercial routes that flow through Havering, to guard these routes against the enemies' plots and schemes, and to allow the flow of good things into the city. This is what gateways do. They are places of permitted entrance and exit. As saints, living in Havering, we have a role to serve in this respect. We need to be aware of what is coming through, and oversee the guarding of this gateway into London, through prayer.

PLACE THREE

THE TWO HAROLDS – GOD'S HONOURED PLACE

Two different communities

Harold Hill and Harold Wood are two very different communities separated by the A12. They are both named after Harold, the last Saxon king born in this area just before the Norman invasion in 1066. This is about the only thing the two Harolds have in common. The community of Harold Wood was built up first around the railway station, as richer people wanted to move out from London into the countryside. Then after the second world war, faced with a huge housing shortage, London City Council bought the farmland beyond the A12 and built Harold Hill, in which the bombed-out families of the east end of London found a home. It was carefully planned as a mixed community with a variety of housing types and green spaces, but quickly became an area of deprivation. The Borough council creates maps, ward by ward of the whole Borough, and the two wards which make up Harold Hill are currently in their highest defined category of deprivation.

Keeping themselves to themselves

On the other side of the A12, I don't think that the people of Harold Wood were very pleased when Harold Hill was built. Rolling farmland had suddenly become acres of social housing. Since then, both communities have kept themselves to themselves. The busyness of the A12 hasn't helped. There aren't many places even to safely cross this road, there is just one main junction connecting the two communities.

God hates division

We felt that the junction between the two communities was the place to sing, and to express how much God wants us to properly honour and respect each another. Whether we are from Harold Hill or Harold Wood, we have been made in the image of God and He has a wonderful plan for our lives. God hates division and fracture, He wants to bring down those who consider themselves high, and lift up those who consider themselves nothing. He doesn't want us to be divided off from one another, with some shunned and excluded. With regards to the church, He wants a proper understanding of who we are in Jesus, and of the dignity and nobility he has bestowed on all of us. So on that special Sunday in June, as the cars stopped and started at the traffic lights, the singers sang at the junction between the two communities, and God spoke about loving and respecting one another.

The A12 junction between the two Harolds

Revival at Hallelujah Corner

God loves to presence Himself in the most unexpected places. Harold Hill, in the early 1950's, had a major moment of revival. Here is the story as told by Margaret Jones, a young girl at the time.

'There was a woman living down the road in Gooshays Gardens. She was the first one to come to the Lord and she was a real soul winner, and so she was telling all her neighbours about it, and she was so different. And her husband wanted to know what had happened to her. And soon the neighbours were coming to the Lord. She was leading them all to the Lord. And she was bringing them into her house, but she didn't know very much to teach them. And so out of all that my father came to Harold Hill as their pastor and started holding meetings in this little council house. And so it built up and up. There was about eighty people meeting there in the end. It was only a little council house!'

God had moved and Gooshays Gardens in Harold Hill became known as Hallelujah corner!

Later the meetings moved into a hall in another part of Harold Hill. In Margaret's words, 'They were wonderful days because all around were prefabs. Oh there was all these children. I mean, they didn't have TV's. They didn't have anything so they used to crowd in! We used to have a Sunday School of three hundred and fifty. They were really wonderful days and the Lord really moved. There were miracles and yes, people were healed. People were saved. It was just amazing!'

Healing of Racial hostility

Clyde Baker, a bishop in the New Testament Church of God, Harold Hill, describes the racial division that God's presence has been healing in the Briar Road area.

'This was a very hostile community against black people. And it was so bad that the pastor before us was unable to have music in the church, unable to pray aloud, and for pleasure they used to break all the glass panes and write up graffiti on the wall. So that was the hostile situation we met, and to see how God changed that so that now people are more friendly and have become more accommodating, and we are in a situation now where that hostility has gone. Really severe hostility to the extent that they would write such graffiti as Niggers go home. When we reported that to Head Office, they couldn't believe it that in this day and age, there would still be people of that ilk... But to see that crossover...There was one gentleman who was really anti to the church, extremely anti.. [This] same guy has become our friend – comes for tea and coffee – [a complete] change of attitude'

God's love embedded in the landscape

This change has come about through the church's patient and generous work in the community. God's love and friendship have been extended. Interestingly, their church meets in the building which Margaret Jones described earlier, as the place where the children flocked to the Sunday School. God's love has been embedded in the landscape in Harold Hill, and all around, there are wonderful testimonies which have been raised up as spiritual markers, to encourage us.

PLACE FOUR

HORNCHURCH - GOD'S PLACE OF POWER

In 1158 the monks of St Nicholas and St Bernard Monastery at Montjoux in Savoy, France were invited by Henry II to establish a priory, here in England, at Hornchurch. Their monastery in Savoy was known as the Horned Monastery, perhaps because it was originally built over a Temple to the goddess Diana, where bull sacrifices were made in Roman times. It may be that the 'Horn' in Hornchurch comes from this past association with the monastery in Savoy, but no-one knows for certain. In 1392, the priory was dissolved and its property and farmlands came under the powerful influence of New College, Oxford. Today, it still holds the patronage of St Andrew's, the local Anglican parish church in Hornchurch, and has the right to choose its vicar. Uniquely this church has a set of bull's horns on its exterior wall.

The power of culture

In the Bible, horns are associated with power, and we felt that Hornchurch was a place that characterised power and influence. Some of the richest residents in the Borough live in this area. We also felt that there was something being declared here, especially about media and culture. Hornchurch is a cultured place. Fairkytes Arts Centre and the Queens Theatre are here. In June 2015, the place from which we chose to sing was on the Green, next to the theatre. This is the place where Passion plays, telling the story about the death and resurrection of Jesus have been held regularly since 1995. We felt it was important to declare Hornchurch as a place of God's power in the media and in our culture.

Hornchurch Passion Play

God is calling people to come out into His freedom and creativity. In the present culture of our nation, distorted understandings of reality are often projected. We believe that God wants us to come away from being affected by these, and instead show people what life can really be like in God's kingdom. The story of how the Passion Play began in Hornchurch is a fantastic witness to God's power to intervene, and bring about cultural changes. It all began with a man in a prayer meeting. Here is Freddy Sayer's story, in his own words, about that moment in 1993.

'In the middle of the prayer meeting, the prayer leader said, "I want us to pray now, and I want us to ask the Lord how we could be used by Him to help build the church. We know the Lord builds the church but He does use us to help Him. So if anyone gets, or thinks they have, a picture or a word from the Lord, then please let me know, and we can pray into that situation". So I thought, Right, OK. It was all new stuff to me so I prayed the prayer. Now my prayer was over in minutes, I just said, "Lord", I closed my eyes, "How can we be best used by you to help you build your church?" Then I opened my eyes and they were all still praying, so I thought, well I better pray again. So I prayed the same prayer over again and opened my eyes again and they were still praying and I remember thinking, "Cor, these are professional prayer people!" So I closed my eyes the third time and this time I found myself outside of my own body, if you like'.

Freddy's vision of Jesus

'I was outside the church, but about forty foot in the air. I wasn't conscious of myself being in the lounge anymore. I was forty foot in the air, looking down on the church. And there were the grounds of the church. I could see people dressed in

Eastern-style dress, like in Jesus' time, but there was a massive fight going on. It looked like a fight, a melee of people punching and kicking somebody. And out of the middle of this crowd, I saw Jesus appear, and Jesus was battered and bruised, and he was carrying His cross, and He walked along the pavement for a bit dragging His cross, and the sense of loneliness I felt at that moment was horrendous!

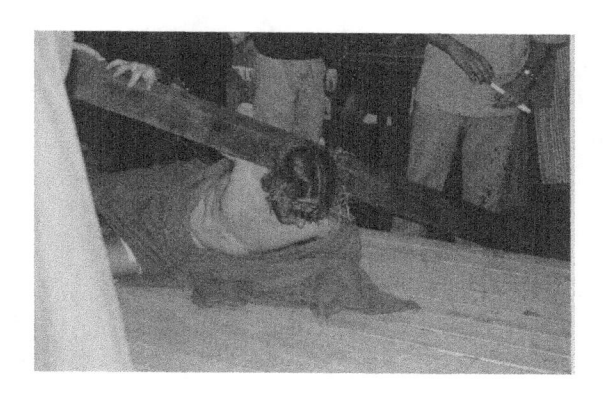

And it touched my heart, and as I watched the Lord walk along with His cross, the scene changed, and it flicked and I found myself, still forty foot in the air, but this time I found myself above Fairkytes in Hornchurch, looking down, with the Queens Theatre to the left of me and the Green to the right. And as I looked down on the Green, I could see Jesus on the cross being crucified. I looked down, and I gasped, and said, "Oh Lord, how could we do this?" I meant, "Lord, how could we do this to you?" Then I got words, and it was a man's voice, very clear, very loud, and it just said to me, "You are to get the people from the Theatre involved." And that was it, I was back in the room. The leader saying, "Did anyone think they heard from the Lord? Did anyone get a picture or a word?" Well I kept quiet just in case they thought I was a bit strange, didn't know what to do, whether to share it or keep quiet or what!... For the rest of the evening I was sort of out of

47

it, out of the prayers, thinking, "Shall I tell?"... I leant across to the leader...I told her what I'd seen. Of course everybody sat back down and they said, "Oh that sounds like a Passion play!"

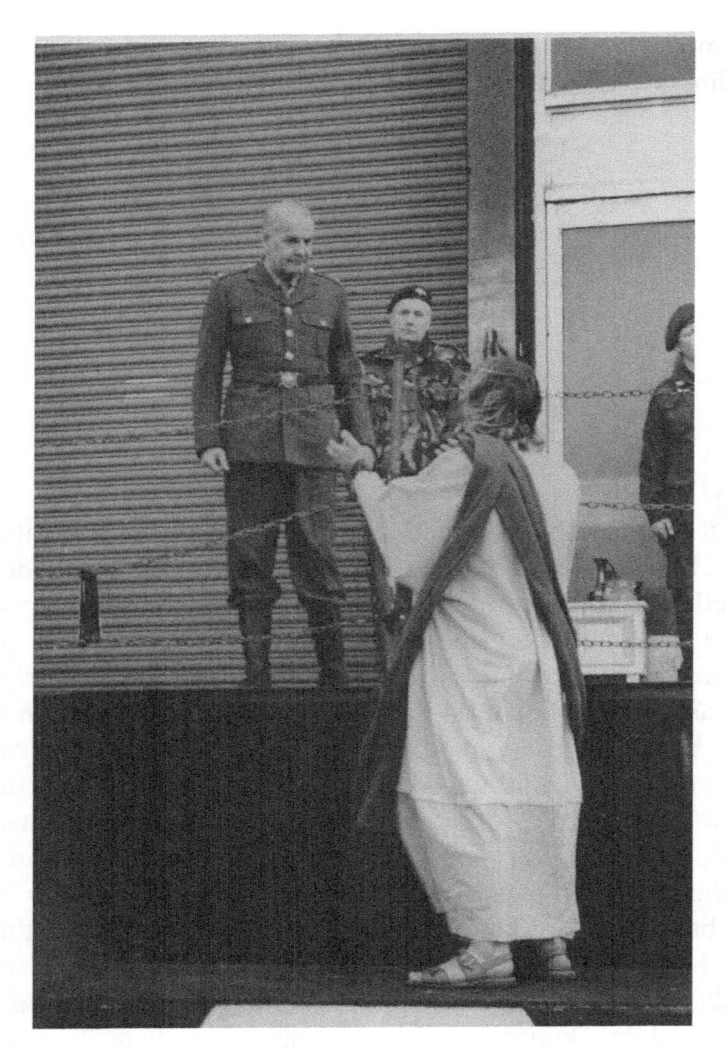

Scene from the Passion play

Queen's Theatre in Hornchurch

The power of the Cross

The foolishness of God is greater than the wisdom of this world. The cross is God's unexpected place of power to forgive sin and defeat death. Following this vision, church leaders across Hornchurch met, and plans for the very first Easter Passion Play on the Green got underway. This has continued every five years or so since, with tremendous impact.

PLACE FIVE

UPMINSTER – GOD'S HOLY PLACE

Scandals and disputes

Upminster is an ancient centre for Christian mission. There has probably been a church on the site of the current Anglican one, St Laurence's, since the seventh century. A quick glance at the history of the Anglican parish church in the last few hundred years, shows that it is one punctuated by disputes. These were mostly over the tithes that local farmers had to pay to the church, but there was also controversy over sexual scandals.

Philip Holden, rector from 1862 to 1904, had an especially colourful history which included him marrying his mistress after her baby was born! He was involved in many legal disputes with locals, including, sadly, one with a local publican over his wife's unpaid drinks bill. She had died an early death from alcohol, and in the last few months of her life had run up a bill which amounted to drinking two bottles of brandy a week! His successor, another Holden, was a major figure in local freemasonry and became the Master of the first lodge in Upminster in 1925. He had hosted its first meeting in the rectory in 1909. When he died in 1944, another Holden took over as rector until 1971. The Holdens just kept holding on! In fact one member or another of the Holden family had been the rector since 1780! During this last tenure by a Holden, yet another freemasons lodge got started in 1944, which met in the church hall.

A call to be totally different

We chose to sing in the centre of Upminster, by the shops, opposite the church, the park and the library. The key word in choosing to sing here was 'opposite'. The Lord wants His people to be the right way up, not in the world's upside down way of thinking. Playing on the word 'Up' in Upminster, and the fact that we chose to stand opposite the library and the church, we felt the Lord saying that here was the place to express that we are called to another way than that of the world. He wants us to go in a totally other direction.

The call to be totally other, is really the call to holiness. Father God has welcomed us into His family, and we no longer belong to this world. In the words of Ephesians chapter two, we once lived that way, 'gratifying the cravings of our sinful nature and following its desires and thoughts' but must do so no longer. To be holy is to be set apart exclusively, for God's purposes. We are also challenged to renew our thinking, not being 'taken captive through hollow and deceptive philosophy which depends on human tradition and the basic principles of this world rather than on Christ (Col. 2:8). Freemasonry, astrology and 'new age' religions, which offer entry into spiritual power through knowledge, all fall into this category.

God wants the church to turn the world on its head! On the day, those singing invited God into Upminster and Cranham. They prayed using Psalm 24:9, that the King of glory would come in, and that the gates of people's hearts would be opened. They prayed specifically against the spiritually deadening effects of Freemasonry.

PLACE SIX
ELM PARK – GOD'S PLACE OF HOPE

A garden city of your dreams

Elm Park was built to appeal to the people who wanted to move out of London into the leafy suburbs. In May 1935, Elm Park Garden City, as it was called, was officially declared open. A new train station had been built, so that workers could commute into London but still live in a country setting, in well-built modern homes with good-sized gardens, and surrounded by fields. The houses were marketed very cleverly, and given wonderful names such as Arcadia and Havenwood. Elsewhere, other builders were just calling their houses Type K or Type X, but not in Elm Park. Here dreams were being marketed. The streets were called names in keeping with the dream. For example we have Woodcote and Northwood. Everything was carefully designed. The kitchens had every modern feature.

New hope offered

Home ownership was being offered with an extremely low deposit (just a pound!). The opportunity to pay back a mortgage over twenty-one years, brought ownership within the means of the working man's pocket. No longer would they have to pay rent all their lives to a landlord and come away with nothing at the end. New hope was being offered. The marketing director promised that with his help the way would be 'made easy for entry upon a fuller and happier life'.

Prospective owners would travel from London onboard free buses and make a day of it, looking round the show houses. The children were entertained too. Disney had just released the film, Snow White, and the builder created a dwarf-sized cottage for them to play in. They employed a fifteen year old girl to be Snow White, and a real dwarf to fish by a pond in the front garden! The first shop in Elm Park was a bike shop which also sold radios. At that time this was everything that people could want. It was a golden era for the bicycle and the radio. The bicycle was affordable transport, the working man's passport to freedom, and the radio, his main source of entertainment!

People brought their problems with them of course. The sense of safety was shattered by Elm Park's first murder in January 1939. A little girl was found dead in a ditch - a murder still unsolved. Then, from 1940 onwards, Hitler started dropping bombs on the place, and towards the end of the war, V1 and V2 rockets with devastating results. After the war, new housing in Romford and Hornchurch exploded into existence all around Elm Park.

Elm Park today

Elm Park is still a nice place to live and has given people a community. They can still walk to the station and commute into London, and there are still some fields on its western side going off towards Dagenham. Thankfully Harrow Lodge Park also forms a strip of green on another side of the community. However 'out in the countryside' doesn't really describe it anymore, and there is much more of suburban sprawl about the area nowadays. In the long term, it didn't quite live up to the expectations of the first happy home-owners.

Our hope is not disappointed.

We chose to sing from the centre of Elm Park, just to the north of the station, by the roundabout. We felt that Elm Park was God's place to express His heavenly promises for Havering, that are Yes and Amen in Jesus. Earthly aspirations may fail, but in Jesus every good desire is fulfilled. Unlike earthly hopes, our heavenly hope is never disappointed in Jesus.

The roundabout in Elm Park

Look up!

There were a lot of pointers in Elm Park to call us to look heavenwards. I find the names of some of the newer churches often point to what God may be saying is significant in an area. A church may choose its name because it wants to identify itself with its community. Sometimes it may choose to highlight a characteristic of itself, or have something prophetic to say about the community it wants to reach. Two of the newer churches in Elm Park have names which point us skywards. Arise Metropolitan Tabernacle and Eagles Christian Connections are both based in Elm Park. So in the words of Isaiah chapter forty, 'let us rise up on eagles wings... and not grow weary'. We have a heavenly hope that will bring us joy, even if we find ourselves weeping until the morning. How interesting that Eagles Christian Connections has planted a church in nearby Hornchurch called Joy Christian Connections. Psalm 16:11 tells us that in God's presence there is fulness of joy and at His right hand there are pleasures forevermore. When we realise God has seated us high up in Heavenly places, we regain our perspective, and joy floods in.

Co-operation and the sharing of resources

When we sang at the roundabout in Elm Park, the Co-operative store was still doing business. Now the Co-op's presence is represented only by their funeral directors, and the shop is trading under a different brand. However, at the time of singing, we did feel that here was a fitting place to express God's desire for His church in Havering to flow in co-operation, and the sharing of resources.

PLACE SEVEN

RAINHAM – GOD'S REMEMBERING PLACE

Remembering those who died

Rainham has a war memorial, unique in the Borough for being a clocktower. There are three clock faces, so the time can be seen from three different angles. Fittingly the bricks are from Belgium, where most of the First World War casualties fell. It was built in 1920, and lists the soldiers who died in both world wars, and also civilians from the Second World War. There was an early rumpus when the local bus company trod on sensitivities and put Rainham clocktower as the name on its timetables, instead of Rainham War Memorial. It was quickly changed.

Rainham war memorial

All over the Borough there are war memorials, remembering those who left their homes never to return. It is fitting too that in Westminster Abbey, there is a National Roll of Honour with the names of the civilians who died in the Second World War. This Roll includes the two hundred and ninety-five civilians from Havering, who died from the bombs and the V1 and V2 rockets. In Havering's final month of V2 rockets, March 1945, over twenty came down and twenty-four people died. Their ages ranged from sixty-eight down to two years old – a little lad called William Oakes. It is very sad when you think that the war in Europe would be over just thirty-eight days later. Peter Watt has catalogued every death in a moving book called Hitler versus Havering.

God knows our names, the times and seasons, and the sacrifice

We chose to sing at the war memorial clock, in the centre of the village, as a place to remember sacrifice. Peter Watt has done a remarkable job in researching and recording those involved in the Second World War in Havering. Recorded by men, for our remembrance, are their name, age, address and the date they died. Elsewhere you can read about what dropped on them, as each bomb's location is meticulously recorded. However there are three telling entries for 19th April 1941 in the name column – three times we read the words, 'known only to God.'

Time may seem as if it is ticking on, but God has a memory. He knows all our names, and the times and the seasons we have been through. He understands the sacrifices, the pain and the sorrow. His intimate knowing of each of us is beyond our measure. The Rolls of Honour, the careful recording of every death, the careful inscribing of name after name on the war memorials across the Borough is nothing alongside His care and loving attention to every detail of our lives.

The oldest church in Havering

God has been giving us His focussed attention ever since Adam and Eve. The Anglican parish church, St Helen and St Giles' is next to the War memorial clocktower, at the centre of the village. This is the oldest church building still standing in Havering, dating from 1160, but is very new from God's point of view! It is quite something to think of different generations worshipping in the place for the last eight hundred and fifty odd years, including me on a few occasions! And God has seen us all, and knows all that we have gone through. Rich or poor, whether lords of the manor or farm workers, we have come through the doors of the church in birth, marriage and death over all that time.

The singers by the war memorial clocktower in Rainham

59

Speaking out words that build up and tear down

He also has a time and a season for everything people involve themselves with. On that Sunday in June when we sang out across Havering, the pray<u>ers</u> in Rainham got a scripture declaring out God's authority over every period of history. In Jer. 1:10 God speaks these words over Jeremiah, 'Today I appoint you over nations and kingdoms to uproot and tear down, to destroy and overthrow, to build and to plant'. God reigns and has a time for everything. He builds up and He tears down. The amazing thing is, that He calls His church to speak out words that have the power to do this. One understanding of the meaning of the name, Rainham is '<u>the dwelling place of the people who rule, the people who prevail</u>.' Our choosing to sing in Rainham reminds us that God calls us, as the church in Havering, to declare the seasons and pray about the building up and the tearing down of the things concerning men. Proverbs 21:30 says 'There is no wisdom, no understanding, and no counsel, that can prevail against the Lord.'

THE EIGHTH PLACE
COLLIER ROW – GOD'S HIDDEN PLACE

Unassuming but totally vital!
Along the edge of the forest in medieval days there was a row of scattered houses lived in by charcoal burners, colliers as they were then called. The trees behind the houses were coppiced, rather than felled, to keep the supply going to make the charcoal. Before coal, charcoal was the main fuel supplying energy, to make the economy work. This row of dirty collier hovels on the edge of the forest was hidden and unassuming and didn't amount to much. Who would think that they were at the birthing end of the whole economic process of the day? The higher temperatures achieved by charcoal made the production of metal tools and weapons possible, for example. The heat from charcoal was used for pottery making and also for lime-burning, which created a type of mortar that was used for building. The outward pomp and grandeur of medieval castles, and their kings, had all started from the dirt and the muck of colliers grubbing about on the edge of the forest. Without the colliers none of the castles could have been built.

God's fire of love inside
There is a hidden energy at work within us. This is the power of God, which like charcoal, provides the fuel for all our outward actions. Paul writes in Colossians 2:29, 'To this end I labour, struggling with all His energy which so powerfully works in me'. Elsewhere in Ephesians 2:20, he prays out, 'Now to Him who is able to do immeasurably more than all we ask or imagine, according to His power that is at work within

us.' Just as the charcoal provided the fuel for the medieval economy, God has put His hidden fire of love within us.

Hidden churches

The surprising general word I got for Collier Row, when Mary and I first came to live here, was just the simple word, 'Hidden'. For me some of the indicators came from my first interactions with the place. It was not an easy task to visit some of the local churches in the area. We drove by several of them, without even spotting them, and even when we knew where they were, we managed to miss them and had to turn around! The first church we visited alternated between two different locations, Sunday by Sunday. We, being new, didn't know that and arrived at a locked door with a notice saying that on this particular Sunday they were at St. So and so's, but there was no address telling us where that was! We went back home. Another local church met in house churches, and it was several weeks before we were given an appointment to visit one of them on a Sunday morning. Other groups were so 'under the radar' that I doubt that anyone new to the area would get to know of their existence. We certainly didn't.

A random pub sign

Later, we were intrigued by the Colley Rowe Inn pub sign in the middle of Collier Row. Hidden, in plain sight, above this local Wetherspoons, on their sign, is a Greek Orthodox icon of a bearded figure with bits of Greek writing on it. This is not the normal thing you'd expect for a pub sign. I'd never seen such a thing and, like Moses with the Burning Bush, it caught my attention. It seemed really random, and no-one seemed to know what it meant or why it was there. The staff didn't, the locals didn't, and when we met for breakfast there as local church leaders one Saturday, none of us knew either. My Greek was a bit rusty, and my translation got as far as one word, bishop. It was a bit hard taking in the rest of the words swinging on the sign high above my head (that's my excuse anyway!).

A hidden patron saint

A few years after this, the Colley Rowe Inn had just been refurbished, and like other Wetherspoons across the country, they had various photos and bits of local history information up on the walls. Mary and I had gone in for a meal and discovered that next, to where we sat down, there was a newly-framed information board about St Alexander of Comana, the patron saint of charcoal burners. It told us that this man had been a charcoal burner. Here was a saint that the medieval charcoal burners of Collier Row knew would understand them. His was the portrait swinging from the sign outside the pub. Clearly in medieval days, this man and his annual feast day in August, would have been a matter of importance to this small community, at a time when life revolved around saints and the church year. For whatever reason, Wetherspoons had decided to highlight this connection with the local Christian heritage of Collier Row by gracing their pub sign with him. Unknown to all of us, Collier Row had its very own patron saint.

Brought out of hiding

What's more the story of Alexander of Comana turns out to be all centred on the theme of a man in hiding. In the days of the Roman Empire, the town of Comana needed a new bishop, and various candidates were paraded before the visiting Archbishop from which he was to choose. They had been picked out from the rich and the noble. However the Archbishop was having none of it, and said that riches and nobility were not the foundational qualities by which to choose a new bishop. Tongue in cheek the 'selection committee' said, 'then you might as well choose this filthy charcoal burner', pointing to Alexander at the edge of the crowd. The Archbishop sensed something about the man, and took him aside and questioned him. He discovered that Alexander was in fact an educated man, who had hidden away in Comana as a charcoal burner, to get away from the worldliness of those around him. Beneath the muck and the grime was a godly man, eminently suitable to become the Bishop of Comana. Washed down, he reappeared, wearing the Archbishop's own cloak as a sign of his new authority.

Don't hide your blessings!

Here was a man who had hidden away. His talents had been neglected, or polished in obscurity, depending on how you want to understand his position, but now God, in due time, had brought him out of hiding. Alexander went on to be an excellent bishop, and was finally martyred in one of the Roman persecutions of Christians, in the second century, aptly but sadly, in a charcoal furnace. The blessing that God intended Alexander to be was no longer hidden away. Enthused by this story, in 2016, on Alexander's feast day, a small team from local churches used the theme, 'Don't hide your blessings day' as a way of interacting with the locals down at Wetherspoons, and sharing with them the message of God's love.

Alexander of Comana Day 2016

More about 'Hidden'

By 'Hidden', I don't mean that you can't find it on a map. This is not about physical geography. Rather Collier Row represents for the whole Borough a positive kind of hiddenness. There are good hidden places in God, from which good things can begin. These are the unassuming thoughts, dreams and the small beginnings that stir up within us. When breathed on by the Holy Spirit, they develop from the inside out and good things are birthed in our personal lives and also, even in our communities and nations. God's hidden place is like a womb within which these good works can gestate. These small beginnings can go on to have massive impacts across the whole world.

Waiting room experiences

A good experience of being hidden can also be likened to a waiting room. There can be times and seasons of waiting in our lives, and the same applies to our communities. There is a time for everything, and some things are left waiting, to emerge at the right moment in God's bigger timetable of history. Sometimes a healing time may be needed after being personally crushed or persecuted. On these occasions, God provides us with spiritual places of hiddenness, to recover ourselves. This can be needed for a church community too. A waiting room time can become a place of healing for a whole church after a major trauma.

Not a tomb but a womb!

Recovering ourselves in a hidden place does not mean burying oneself, or allowing others to nail down a coffin lid over our lives. There is certainly an experience in the Christian walk of dying daily, but God calls us through this experience into His abundant life, not into a tomb. We are called to walk by faith, not to hide in fear and intimidation. Jesus said, 'The enemy comes to steal, kill and destroy'. We are not to believe any lies that our lives are worthless and don't amount to much. Collier Row doesn't represent a hiding place of fear and unfruitfulness. At the risk of alliteration, God's hidden place isn't a tomb but a womb, or a waiting room! In God's hidden places, there is a flow of life and fruitfulness.

A hidden field waiting for rain

There is a hidden field in Collier Row. You would have to google-map it to spot it on satellite view, if you wanted to satisfy yourself that it really was there. You certainly couldn't see it from the ground as you walk through the streets. Behind the houses on Moray Way and Wallace Way, completely hidden from sight from an earthly viewpoint, is this hidden field.

It is buried in the geography but not hidden from God. Surprisingly it has an important job to do as a floodplain for the area. Its whole job is to wait there for the rain. If more rain than normal happens it acts as a safety valve place, where the excess water can be released. It may look like a mistake has been made, and a piece of land has been forgotten, hidden behind the houses, but this field is exactly where it should be, and the local residents ought to be very grateful it's there. For me it is an indicator that God can do wonderful things through hidden unassuming places. In the hidden place He has made His church ready, to handle the pouring rain of revival.

Hidden songs

In the early days of the house church movement, in the 1970s, a number of Christians gathered here in Collier Row. They were hidden in the physical sense, and many may not have been aware of them at first. Houses were bought in Wilton Drive, and families began to model what it means to be a prophetic community. From this hidden place, an impact has been made that has gone way beyond the boundaries of the Borough! For example, many new worship songs have been birthed here which have gone on to be sung around the world. These include songs such as 'Abba Father let me be yours and yours alone', and 'Bind us Together, Lord'. When we sing worship songs, very few of us think about who penned the song, and when and where and why it happened. However, we should be very thankful to God for the songs that are being written. They are coming out of someone's hidden times of intimacy with God.

A good place to begin from

With regards to our singing over Havering in June 2015, I felt it was apt that Collier Row was the place we all set out from. The seven worship groups officially started out from the Methodist church in Collier Row, and came back there later that Sunday afternoon. It was from this eighth place that we waved off the others. This fits in well with Collier Row representing new beginnings. Biblically, eight bears this significance of new birth, new starts, new life and new beginnings. For example, there were eight people who stepped out from the ark, to begin a new life after the flood. Another example is the gematria of Jesus' name itself, the number that characterises him. This, when counted up from the Greek letters in Jesus, comes to 888. Jesus is the author of Life, the firstborn of a new creation. How fitting then that His numbered name should be full of eights.

The Church is at war!

We also thought the date of our singing was rather cool. By choosing Sunday 7th June, we had picked the anniversary weekend of the D-Day landings in Europe, during the Second World War. Though not at all on the same scale, it was a good reminder that the church is engaged in its own form of warfare, and that there is an enemy to stand firm against. We felt it was an appropriate moment to be declaring God's songs over Havering, against all the dissonance and cacophony of evil.

Unity, Renewal and healing

While the others went their different ways to the seven locations around the Borough, a small group of us walked down through the Havering Park estate in Collier Row to Bacon Link. This is a small road between two parts of the estate where a bridge carries the road over the River Rom and links the Estate together. From here the Rom flows down to the River Thames, being renamed the Beam River further downstream after Romford. A lot of renewal work is being done right now and a conservation group has been set up to help further this work.

The River Rom in Collier Row

A flowing river full of life

We sang out from the bridge because we considered this to be an appropriate place of connection, and prayed for unity not division in our community. We prayed for spiritual renewal for the whole community, that people would come to know God's salvation.

The physical renewal of the river seems like a tangible visible indicator of the spiritual renewal, that God desires to do in human hearts all over the area. He has a river flowing to bring healing, whether physical, emotional or relational.

The Rom doesn't always look much like a river. In places you might be misled into thinking that it looks no more than a large ditch, but this is not the case. It is a flowing river and is full of life. We need to see with God's perspective, the life already here! God is at work in Havering bringing unity, renewal and healing. We want His light to shine forth, His beams of light to flow out through Romford. We want Him to take the nondescript and ordinary and change us into His kind of river. The River Rom becomes the Beam River. In Jesus, we all get to have a name change, and become beams of light shining out God's goodness.

PART THREE

GRASSROOTS AND OPEN WELLS

GRASSROOTS AND OPEN WELLS

A 'Together' Body of Christ
Gary Seithel, from Across Havering, a forum for church and ministry leaders across the Borough, said these words recently at a large worship gathering we called Open Wells. 'We are a Together body of Christ. We are seeing the vision of the streams flowing together in Havering and wider, bringing people together from a wider area to have the same heart, to grow together, to worship our one true Christ, our one true God – the Lord Jesus Christ who is exalted and fills the whole universe - but He fills you and He fills me. And as He fills us, we'll overflow, water will spill out on everyone around us... that's my prayer'.

Spring up, O Well!
I love to go to a spring called St Cedd's Well in North Ockendon, a small hamlet just within the Borough. It bubbles out into a big lake, which doubled up as a moat for a manor house at one time. The house has gone, but the water is still flowing out into the lake. You can't prove it historically but this is where, we believe, thousands of our Essex ancestors got baptised by St Cedd, an apostle sent to this region from Northumbria in the seventh century. So we're talking about the Christian message hitting our ancestors about fourteen hundred years ago! We are thankful for people like Cedd who came and risked their lives preaching the gospel, so that our ancestors might come to know Jesus.

God's work at grassroots level
When I go to St Cedd's well, I sense God isn't finished with Havering. Just as words of hope and life were sung out then to the people being baptised, God continues to fulfil every good word spoken out now. God has placed giftings within us that

not only bless us, but also get the gospel out to the whole community. This is a grassroots thing. Just as local water is bubbling out from the underground water table at the well, so God has a hidden flow of life flowing out from within us, the life of the Holy Spirit. The well is open. In John 7:38, Jesus tells us, 'Whoever believes in me, as the scripture has said, streams of living water will flow from within him.' Let us encourage each other that God is at work from the grassroots outwards. He wants us to see with the eyes of the Spirit our common local geography. He sees the church with joined-up thinking. From His presence within us, as His church in Havering, there is hope and freedom flowing out to others.

St Cedd's well

To conclude...

On Sunday 7th June 2015, we went out with God's songs of blessing and sang at seven locations in Havering from an eighth location in Collier Row. During the afternoon God was expressing His own song through us. The song that we sang together has something to say to us about how to be as the church in Havering. We believe that God wants us to learn and grow in our relationship with Him, from the things we have prophetically expressed in this book about each location. Here are His words for us.

Out of the hidden place of <u>intimacy</u> (Collier Row) let us spend time at
- the royal place (Havering-atte-Bower)
- the spacious place (Romford)
- the place of honouring (Harold Hill and Harold Wood)
- the place of power (Hornchurch)
- the holy place (Upminster)
- the place of hope (Elm Park)
- the place of remembering (Rainham).

God has been ordering the landscape, lining things up spiritually and selecting what to put into place for this time in the Borough. The worshippers, the prophets and the pray<u>ers</u> are all needed. An atmosphere of revival is being nurtured. God wants us to trust in Him and keep going. He hasn't abandoned us, we are no longer orphans. We are joining in with what our Father God has been doing over the generations, and He is good at what He does.

If you live elsewhere than Havering, God is likewise calling you to take a fresh look at your area. He is inviting you to go on a new journey with Him, with eyes to see and ears to hear.

Our prayer is that the Holy Spirit within you will show you what to sing out in the area where you live.

Some references:

The Elm Park story, Chris Hipperson, Simon Donoghue and Ingrid Brandon 2009

Hitler versus Havering, Peter Watt 1994

Romford, Collier Row and Gidea Park, Brian Evans 1994

Clyde and Merle Baker; Matt Carter; Margaret Jones and Freddie Sayer - Interview transcripts made by Bob and Mary Bain in 2016

God on the Move documentary – a Welcome Network film, available as a DVD 2017, see welcomenetwork.org for details.

My Song Matters – A book of Poems, Mary Bain 2015

Bob and Mary Bain

BOOKS FROM OPEN WELLS PUBLISHING

BY THE SAME AUTHORS

Becoming Multi-flavoured Church

My Song Matters – a book of poems

Singing over Havering

Prayer Walking around Redbridge

Available from www.lulu.com or Amazon